THOSE APRIL FEVERS

Other titles by Mary O'Donnell

POETRY
Reading the Sunflowers in September
(Salmon Poetry, 1990)
Spiderwoman's Third Avenue Rhapsody
(Salmon Poetry, 1993)
Unlegendary Heroes
(Salmon Poetry, 1998)
September Elegies
(Lapwing Press, 2003)
The Place of Miracles, New & Selected Poems
(New Island Books, 2005)
The Ark Builders (Arc Publications, 2009)
[as co-editor]
To the Winds Our Sails
an anthology of Galician women's poetry
(Salmon, 2010)

FICTION
Strong Pagans (1990)
The Light-Makers (1992 & 1993)
Virgin and the Boy (1996)
The Elysium Testament (1999)
Storm Over Belfast (2008)
Where They Lie (2014)

MARY O'DONNELL
Those April Fevers

2015

Published by Arc Publications
Nanholme Mill, Shaw Wood Road
Todmorden OL14 6DA, UK
www.arcpublications.co.uk

Design by Tony Ward
Printed in Great Britain by TJ International, Padstow, Cornwall

978 1908376 57 2 (pbk)
978 1908376 58 9 (hbk)
978 1908376 59 6 (ebook)

ACKNOWLEDGEMENTS

Thanks are due to the following print and online journals and
anthologies, as well as to RTE Radio, where some of this work has
appeared: *2012: Twenty Irish Poets Respond to Science in Twelve Lines;
Agenda; Breac; Cyphers; Estudios Irlandeses* (ed Rosa Gonzalez);
*Festschrift on Maurice Harmon's 80th birthday; The Irish Times; New
Hibernia Review* (The University of St. Thomas, Saint Paul, USA);
Outburst; Poethead (poetry blog); *Poetry Ireland Review; The Prairie
Schooner; Revista Audem* (ed. Elena Jaime); *Skylight 47* (Galway); *South
Bank Poetry* (London); *The Stinging Fly; Stony Thursday Book* (Limerick);
Studies Irish Quarterly Review; Sunday Miscellany (RTE Radio); *The
Warwick Review; What We Found There: poets respond to the treasures of
the National Museum of Ireland.*

Thanks are also due to the Centre Culturel Irlandais, Paris, for a
welcome residency in 2012 during which some of these poems were
composed.

Cover photograph: Mark Granier

**Editor for the UK and Ireland:
John W. Clarke**

for Aunt Mary O'Donnell

CONTENTS

BALTIC AMBER

Someone said I would uncover pieces of amber
from long-dead trees on this Baltic shoreline.
Day by day, I leave the cottage, walk the sands
to a headland village.

Nobody understands
what I mean when I mention amber, their minds
engrossed by hazel branches hung
with painted eggs, catkins; or hyacinths in bowls.
The time for hyacinths is long gone, I tell them.

I am in need of something that has survived
more than winter, hardening to translucent gold,
enclosing – perhaps – one small seed,
to honour the month and the Easter I was conceived.

I have grown six decades, like aeons,
and my tears have surely become like amber,
enriched and smooth, taking tawny colours
for blood.

Next week I will be casual
about the search, will uncover nuggets
beneath tree fragments,
inhaling salt and resin as I turn freely
from eggs, catkins, those April fevers

WAKING

These mornings you make peace with throwing in the job,
bend over my pillow, kiss me. I swim in the blue

of your eyes, could be that new bride, the one
you imagined you'd married, treasure you risked your life

to bring back to shore from some foreign place.
We always jumped land and ship, never quite at home.

Now we are here, peculiar to ourselves with buoyancy
and roots, ship and shore again for the taking.

Shore is wilder than you thought, shell reefs catch your eye,
a place where mermaids gossip in moonlight,

their dusky nipples, sea-green cleft of tail,
salt-white hair – all imagined in your absence into being.

But journeys did not part us, nor working contradictions
of our tuning. That jangle gave some purchase to the task.

It has taken so long to draw you to this cottage,
across the sands. Wake now. Wake to new doing,

to new pauses in new days. I cannot sleep for joy.
Mermaids no longer bathe in moonlight but you are here.

Sometimes, I miss their gossip, tasks they set
that became my pleasure. See my breasts, the dusky nipples,

two strong legs, my sea-green toenails, and remember:
your ship, but this my shore, created in your absence.

BEYOND MYTHS

Only you can look me in the eye
and hold my gaze. After all these years,

only you return the look.
I'm indifferent if the others look away.

Occasionally, they hesitate on Stephen's Green
or Merrion, as if a ghost reminded them

of something half-forgotten, still
hankered for. Yes, it's me, I whisper,

passing by, my need long stanched
for them or sly-eyed lines –

Botticelli Venus, white witch,
Rapunzel in her tower.

They've faded to a past in which
we played in passion's house,

blind to where it really lives. Now,
only you can look me in the eye,

and want to, only you can see the shape
beyond the myths.

PLEASURE PRINCIPLES

The audio's turned high.
I press the accelerator,
Rachmaninov in my ear.

The motorway rolls out,
time's chute drawing me faster
as chords and road signs build, break

above the sounds of engine, and the wind buffets
the windscreen with quick fists,
and I'm alive to the wet crush of this music.

Later in the restaurant,
sight also pinpoints to the look of you,
my nose a bouquet

of dog-like discrimination
at our perfect meal, that perfumed wine,
or the twist of sheets when we unbundle our secrets.

Mouth still searches the oasis of your skin,
I become cataract, falling champagne,
taken on the tongue.

With its trillion pores, collective apertures
of the body's wall,
a habitation. I take pleasure through skin,

quietly as a dawn swim
before the other tourists see this naked ageing
child at play; and I take pleasure

mirror-wise, see all as it should be,
        steady on shuffle journey down time's alley,
where already, something waits,

those just-born stars. Fizzing.

Young nurses will decipher the lives of those
who enjoyed the pin-drag and burn of needle,
the blue and the black and the green inks.
They will know the once open secret of Wayne's love
for Suzy, also daubed on a water silo near the railway,
and of his love for Mum. They will note how Emma's
shoulder-heart meant she too had felt the pain;
then the leaping strength of Jake's red dragon,
its fires of justice, still reflected in his ageing mind.
All that rippled across the enclosing sheath
of our lives, crinkles like loosed silk, then sags.
Each sponging down, each soothing powder
settles on the erasing moment:
evening, pills, and night's obliteration,
a patient laying out as colour is consumed.

DRIVING INVISIBLE THROUGH A WORLD OF MIRRORS

From house to world
I come, I go,
unwrap time's latest offering,
merely curious at such plain boxing.
More mirrors, I grumble,
as if I had not enough.

I spin within the revolving doors
of this building or that,
the mirror-box beneath my arm,
knowing I enter or exit unreflected,
that the woman behind,
purple button boots clipping
granite pavement, is busily blind
to a shade like me; or the man with a belly,
in no position to cast his net,
would fish that young one to spear her
on the surface of his own pond.

Through the car window, the mad,
moving world breaks up
in rivulets of rain, as if
the Liffey rose skywards
on shaky green legs.
I cannot object, once again cast a glance
at the unadorned packaging,
the ribbon-less, brown box
gifted by my honourable suitor Time.
Despite his little mirrors,
the years ahead seem carelessly bright,
wet, so free.

I start. I brake.
I speed. I slow.
Enter. Exit.
Come. Go.

MARRIAGE ADVICE, 1951

Glossy women made her tremble,
every word shiny and sure,
we're going to give Jenny a make-over,
Jen, the decaying building,
the clueless relic.

They made her sweat, even more,
those women with Dior skirts
and nipped-in waists, who warned
the night before the wedding
about being prepared.

But it was 1951. Next day,
she tried not to faint at the altar
although the neighbours whispered,
later forced herself to stuff
some morsel of the wedding breakfast
through her lips, like bad language
or something a woman never did
masticate, masticate, chew, chew, swallow,
the fist of the still-hidden child
walloping her gorge as the best man rose,
twinkle-eyed, yellow card in hand,
a twist of jokes she'd be bound to appreciate.

SPRING FUNERAL

We move as actors in the family opera, sing our best
and worst roles. Sparrows nest in the belfry,

lilac trembles beneath gusted cloud. Grief plays some part,
and other things not intended for a funeral.

There's Lear, raging at the loss of all held dear,
while Fool son, despised, points again to the error of his ways.

There's Daughters Elder and Younger, united
as they move across the nave towards Cousin, prefecting

and bright-eyed, never more alive as she consoles.
Also Unwanted Uncle whose crime is never clear,

Maiden Aunt who remembers the crime though also his birthday.
There too, Middle Child, a trembling veil over her eyes,

the skewer of her unhappiness in a tight percussion of heel-beat,
as she fills the church from door to pew. And then

the walk from church to grave, as one and all divided.
We cluster around a naked rectangle, fall silent

as the coffin lowers. The whole earth sings a clattering aria
as clods crumble on wooden lid, repeats the lines

to the beat of our hearts: one day, understudy, the next,
the curtain call we always knew would come.

AT A WEDDING, THE STRANGER

At the wedding, the stranger, believing
she was Marilyn incarnate, shimmered
in a pea-green skirt that licked at her hips
in the August breeze, her buttocks glossed
and pawed by light that handled her
as a man might. Family eyes fastened
to her every move, the slightly parted mouth,
her lacy, gloved fingers, the netting
that shivered over her face, but
did not conceal the spark from sheen-lidded,
dark, pupils. Uncles, brothers, nephews, fathers,
paused, suspended in a dream some remembered,
or thought they did. Believing in Marilyn,
believing in this stranger as if the part
of the Virgin Mary one never spoke of
was suddenly exposed for their eyes only.
The stranger danced and laughed,
then kissed the bride and made her way
from marquee to taxi. She trailed a silk scarf
like a flag, then floated off up the hill.
The men blinked into wakefulness,
turned again to their wives.

VIEW TOWARDS A BRIDGE

after Hiroshige's 'Sudden Shower Over Shin-Ohashi Bridge and Atake', 1857

Mid-way across, the sky opens. People
look up, puzzled, then hurry. Rain fixes
in fine lines between cloud and river, pinions
the small humans, hampering every step.
Coats and umbrellas are useless. Girls' dresses,
men's shirts suck close to skin, the patterning
in livid tattoos as the sky unyarns.
People stick in the warp like knots,
but the bridge arches like thick weft,
bears their weight.
The man I watch for stops
in his tracks as if to say 'No further!',
snaps shut a black umbrella, leans over
the wooden rail. Sheltered in Moon-viewing
Point, I see how rain has darkened his blue
suit, how the heavens smudge cobalt ink across
his shoulders. He is thinking. I wait,
see his mind at work, knowing
it is not the downpour, nor clouds,
not the height of each spindle of moisture,
nor greyness on the far shore where trees
crumble to the water, nor the chalcedony
blue of the lake where the stiles of the bridge
plunge down, that make him pause.
Drenched, he gazes waterwards,
and my heart tightens – too hot, too dry –
my tongue, alive with news for him,
turns to stone in my mouth, as I realise
he is thinking of me.

MOON VIEWING POINT

after Hiroshige

After the others departed, we looked at the moon.
It was the purpose of this place, after all.
The small boats, like the lit souls of the just born
and just dead, shivered far out on the water.
We saw a million dancing moons when the wind
chivvied the lake. Then it calmed again,
revealed a moon in sky and in water,
one as real as the other. Oyster light
undressed our skin, there was paleness
and shadow, our voices too, low and secret
from one who hesitated behind the screen,
her silence anxious as she set down
bowls of sweet rice, and fish.

WOMAN, 1950

after Willem De Kooning

"There is a contrast between the delicacy of the dessein of de
Kooning and his dreadful women. On one side, poetry of lines
and colors, on the other side provocative vulgarity and ugliness.
I wouldn't be surprised to find in one of his works a case of
vagina dentata."
                    Uploaded anonymously, 4 August 2008, on YouTube.

Why do they have to paint us with hockey balls for breasts
or else like this – splayed downwards, oblong as marrows
from gravity and overuse? In their hands,
what happened to our faces? Vile teeth, mad eyes, mouths
incapable of anything much beyond rage?
As for our crotches? These jagged, spiky triangles
with a gash of red, seem downright dangerous.

Who is the woman whose body is scraped to life
as pummelled quadruped on mangled sheets? The viewer
is free to imagine the loose bulk of breasts
created from Alizarin Crimson, Titanium White,
if only they could touch. Others would hold knives
and razors to slash that tickling fizz of hair back
from her face, while conspiring fingers
rake through the glistening rawness he has exposed below.
This is not apples in bowls, and those grinning teeth
are set in mouths eternally open to a bite, a scream.

HOCKNEY

Hockney has painted the world with invisible joys and boys,
with blue pools into which we have all, gladly, dived
to cool ourselves from the Californian sun;

Hockney loves cats – we know this – especially Percy,
scion of Mr. and Mrs. Clark, all caught in
the spectacular stillness of youth and early marriage;

Hockney's plants lean eternally towards the sun,
in bristling good health as yellow ochre and burnt sienna
spill annunciating grace on chlorophyll, and the blue slats

of summer shutters are heard to crack quietly in heat.
Hockney adores Stanley and Boodgie, his dachshunds,
immortalising his friends in yellow and blue.

Now Hockney is home to paint the Wolds,
and dreamers like me want to live in his landscapes,
beneath blue, furling trees, long nibs of cut wood,

where the ground is not merely green, but purple
with bluebells and clover, and the seer in such a land
would tumble daily in the peculiar logic of nature;

Hockney is home again. I don't want him to paint me.
I want to be his paint. It's the only way
I'll ever stay alive, swinging from the tree of life,

somewhere in the Wolds.

A PEASANT WEDDING

after Pieter Brueghel the Younger

The bride's short neck has vanished
beneath plump chin and crowned head.
What she thinks of the feasting
is anybody's guess: so many courses

transport the guests from everyday
coarse breads, turnip, and salt pork
that lasts the winter. This
is the best they can imagine:

soup of stewed cabbage
with cinnamon and cloves,
a display of fresh boar's head,
oysters and soft white bread,

summer's finest fruits, pitchers of ale,
then honey from the groom's own hive,
a cake that fills, its saturated apples
brimming with the sugars of Paradise.

Racked by compliance and fear,
the bride's sweating thighs clamp together,
as she smells gluttony within the barn
– for food, for sex – and yet more beer.

The others dance or court, the men's knives
at ease below their belts, while codpieces
protrude carelessly. Her aunt and uncle
snarl like curs over a piece of bread,

the aunt's sharp nose pinked from years of weather,
her husband's fist set to win the tug of war.
One or two are removed, by drink
or melancholy, while one lowly fellow

24

fidgets with his fingers in distraction.
Yet distraction abounds, the other kind,
where, for a day, all bellies are packed and taut,
blood courses beneath skin, a sun-warmed river,

and for two conspiring women, words
are a grace-filled balm of knowledge
poured on one another's wounds.
Even the musicians have stalled,

although the dancers have not missed
the strum of string, honk of horn
that roused them some three hours ago.
At the end, the guests will fade in clusters

or in twos, calling back some mirthful quip,
the night not yet over, they imply,
for bride and groom, who must begin
that most mysterious of lives,

imprisoned within seasons, the harsh,
cross weft of land-labour
and many births, and the long scythe
that clears their field each autumn.

In the physics lab, Stephen announces String Theory
for the uninitiated. His eyes shine, as he articulates
connectedness, where one quark to the left of our heads
lies possibly another universe, with people who also
babble, discuss coffee brands and world violence.
But that assumes likeness, he warns.
I do not heed him. Why shouldn't it
blaze on us, diverse and unalike as asphodel
and knitted sheets, marbles and rugby balls,
alien-multiversal and at odds with us?

Great CERN, tubular metal spider, fills her belly
with space, she is clean and fast,
a sprint from breakthrough.
But outside the lab, the boughs of lime-trees
swing up, swing down. For a moment,
dark energy and ground-pull contest the wind.
Stephen looks at me. Electrodynamics and matter
are one thing, he says, it's gravity that baffles.

CHRONICLE OF THE OIL WARS

Every generation believed itself the worst,
the trains unhealthy, electricity evil.
Then pylons were a menace,
giant electro limbs marching across fields,

causing depression, psychosis, stillbirths.
In the end they conformed to electricity,
bought cheap oil. Then the grumbling
about expanding fields, farmers gutting hedges – haw,

hazel, ash – for the sake of wheat for Europe – burnt
stubble each autumn after the field was used,
those raw-bearded genital acres,
flensed by fire before replanting.

Mice and pygmy-shrews fled to the edge
where old cats waited their chance.
Those threshing machines ran on oil, it had to be good.
Yet there was worse. Oil sucked from coastal deeps

in thick, anaconda-like pipes, the dead fish
strewn like Chinese curses on the surface,
birds coated as if with molasses, shellfish
rotting in a sludge of burst intestine

below hopeless reefs. Still they bred children,
released from wombs in sweet,
mysterious oils, in retrospect
thinking pylons not so bad, nor force-feeding

wheat fields till they could yield no more,
not even the Oil Years in the early twenty-first,
when the sea moiled liquid tar. Oil was everywhere:
in water, in war, oiliness mixed with everything,

so that nobody noticed when the streets became oil,
the windows oil, the schools oil, the children
oil too, the certificates needed to get jobs
were oil, cars, bikes and contraceptives were oil,

national boundaries were oil, continents were oil
and deserts that once were sand became oil,
and the hooves of camels were oil, and the Emirati
were oil, The Empty Quarter, Rub al Khali was oil,

the trade routes now spiceless, just oil,
and presidents great and small, faithful to their wives
or not, fat or thin, were oil, spoke a language
that was oil, all oil, so that the planet orbited

to the glub of one sound only:
oil   oil   oil   oil

SEA LIFE IN ST. MARK'S SQUARE

The fish are visiting sunken cities,
        the legendary watropoles,
                They move across brows of mountain ranges,
                        to unlaced canals, above crumbling walls
                conservators fretted over; where people
        broke for lunch in a clatter of trattorias,
photographed pigeons, or drifted, in love:

one of the first casualties, quick-swamped when
        the Adriatic bowl overflowed. Now,
                Cetacean travellers go where no human dared:
                        scale the limpid waters of cathedral domes,
                blowholes closed until they next break surface.
        Here, abundance – church-reefs and palaces
for purple clams, where sea-anemonae,

corals, also build and bloom, breathy
        in the light of thick water. Daily visitors arrive
                from the Barrier Reef, or the Galapagos,
                        porpoises leap and skitter around the
                lightning conductors of the Campanile,
        the seals in San Marco tower frolic as,
even now, bells attempt sound, a low groan,

dismal and drowned. New order spider-crab
        scuttles and flicks on street floors, avoids
                lurking octopus in a Medici urn,
                        angling for the island of Murano,
                at one with the colour of glass.
        In St. Mark's, the basilica crumbles,
the ravens have melted in chloride, bromium,

into knots of sea-wrack. Occasional tsunamis
affect little, sporting moments for the fringe-footed
or finned to surf the ocean
as we once did – a memory of ourselves
we shall never know,
being now microscopic,
on the backs of barnacles encrusting the bells.

MAPPING EUROPE AFTER GLOBAL WARMING

They grew up on an island,
looked to the big bones
of other countries, arteries of rivers,
the thousand-acred fields, pinnacled cities –
proof of a different history in museums
and echoing galleries.

Such places once drew the islanders away
from their sea-slobbered land.
Now the ice-shelf's drifting.
On the land mass they discover
how it felt to be an islander.

Flood-plains of Danube and Rhine
submerge roads, dredge towns flat,
tideless places are prey to moon-drag,
new seas sluice the olive-shaded hills.

Road, bridge, poplar and cypress
slide and crumble; once summery homes
of the Alpes Maritimes are lifted,
to bob like floating toys on the surging sea.

Survivors new to island life
wonder what settlements remain,
what rivers on which to sail.
It begins again: the passion for escape,
for what is bigger, freer, their thoughts defined
by scraps of memories that magnify by the hour,
thoughts of the nudging fellowship
of crowds, what might deliver their children
to imagined excellence.

It is not like an earthquake, not like drought.
Worse – water breaking continents
to pour itself across the land.
It bucks and flashes wetly,
a mirror for the sun.

GOTH PERSEPHONE'S MOTHER ASKS HER
TO DO THE MESSAGES

Persephone dear, run you on out, bear the buds with care,
they've wintered deeply and today you must dress
      the season.
Over there, drab hedges in need of blackthorn studs,
the chain metal of early dew, cast your tattooed arms
over the chestnut, it's wind-chilled since the high hedge
was cut, alone on the field's edge, you'd wonder
at the man that sprays and plants, so that sister earth
has scarcely a breath between seasons.

But run you on out Persephone, gently, mind,
along the gardens, along night streets
where cherries tremble, and rowans
fear the boys with knives and needles,
alone since the older men have left on journeys,
sequestered behind high walls, foot-deep metal doors.
The lads need us, you flooring them in black boots,
skirt flouncing your hips, make-up like poppy pollen,
shove it up the nose of spring till she snorts it high.

Fill these baskets Persephone dear, to the windy streets
of cities, towns, rush on to where the young are deserted,
we must not fail, then play a concert in yellow and purple,
our optimistic tartans, bagpipes of the branches
hailing life in sun and rain, wee birds on the march
and singing contrapuntal. Away with you, Persephone,
lift the garment of spring, bloomers and g-strings,
slips and dangling under-things on every tree, hedge, field,
bannering out this morning across the provinces!

SUMMER EVENING

It is August, and the flies are zipping
to and fro, gnats spin in furious loops,

while five swallows tilt their wings,
perpetual between hedge and sycamore.

I find my prayer within the stillness,
no longer separate from tree, swallow,

midges. I feel – love – alive
in this jubilant release from want,

that quiet grief, twin of the breaths
and heartbeats of our days.

I trace the road back to the setting world,
a silky swish of feather on my soul.

BUZZARD

Came August, it furrowed beneath the sun,
above the big field, low enough to sight
the scallop of wing-tip, that opaque span
widening as it steadied in a downwards
sweep. Sometimes it sat on electric cables
that festooned and crackled across the sky,
shouldered in on itself briefly, a pause
to fall to flight, resume that longing cry.

It cut like scythes beneath cloud-trails,
sky-pirate circling the garden during stolen,
golden days. We were never too lost
in sunbathing, or unrubbling new potatoes,
to look up and up, measuring the distance to
a world that tilted savagery from its cup.

PLEASURE

Slack and easy as dropped sails, the rook's wings:
on the high bank beneath the trees, sun melted
deeply into the stiff mail of every feather.
Warmth penetrated to flesh. The black head
arched, shivered, eyes attentive to the sky,
dark sails of wing silky beneath shoulders,
on this noon-lit grassy slope, freed to rest.
The bird, scarcely visible from the passing car

stretched and quivered in the outspread slumber
of a cosmos indifferent to itself –
sat softly pleasured on grass, yet frail too
despite mail of feather and stone-hard beak,
in the respite of heat, the wings at rest,
shuddering, first summer out of the nest.

WAITING
(SCHOOL ROAD, STRAFFAN, 2002)

It has grown, not darkly, like mould, that sunless green. Sitting
provides the habit of air. Children – trees, coats, limbs,
the bounce of long hair as they troop the school road –

means stillness, expansion, despite unspeakable radio news
on the murder of infants in temperate suburbs. Muffled,
    gloved,
I grow in a car at the end of an eight-year planting, half of me

mulling the latest distant shooting. I would like to book a flight,
transplant skills, solutions, get there fast. Instead, I wait, the smell
of cooked dinner impregnating denims, boots, my cap, which she

inhales as she steps inside the car. I hold myself together
beneath iced winter branches in grey *couteur,* feel an invisible
frieze of buds stirring slowly in deep cold.

FEEDING THE CRONE

The crone is knocking on my door.
Despite myself I open.
A north wind gusts in.
'Any chance of a cup of tea?'
she asks, conciliatory,
(as if we hadn't been through this rigmarole
several times already).

I wouldn't grudge a person
the chance to wet their lips,
I'd throw in a biscuit or two,
not to mention a slice of the cake
my daughter made yesterday. That's
what she needs! A young girl's cake,
duck eggs and spelt flour, nutmeg
and bitter butter, her generous finger-sifts.

I slip the crone a huge triangle,
knowing she won't say no.
Blue and white frosting sidle
down the sides, stick to her fingers,
make their way to sweeten her mouth.
She swallows and licks,
casts a glance at the cake a second time.
Again, I cut deep, to fill her sagging
belly. What else would I do?
By the time she's done,
she hesitates in the doorway,
a smile almost cracking her jowls.
'That was some cake,' she whispers,
turning away, patting herself
as if she was pregnant.

THE ARTISTS ARE SLEEPING

The artists of Ireland are sleeping tonight.
While the birches learn once again to reveal themselves,
strip to marbled bark as winter rides in, the artists

are cocooned in their duvets, down pillows
beneath their heads, (it is said). Some keep notebooks
by the bed (just in case), others sleep in a garden workshop,

beside unfinished canvas, in a tangle of clothes
on a camper bed. The dancers' feet and knees
twitch to the cycle of sleep, while young composers

face nightmares of the one out-of-tune
instrument in an entire orchestra.
The novelists snore through plot changes,

the double-narrative of breathing and near suffocation
for the long hard road to an ending.
Short story writers have a primmer time of it,

curl like hedgehogs, hands like small paws
tucked beneath chins as their cells
shed the prickle of over-stating the case.

Only the poets never truly sleep,
restless in REM, the sieves of their imaginations
still sifting language from muddy waters.

They lie prone on pillows of stone,
bardic to the last, unable to forsake
the fever and fret, circadian rhythms ill-tuned

for orderly living. They shred themselves to the core,
their open hands offer words as the only covering
when winter rides in to circle the birches.

THE WORLD IS MINE

1 July 2014

From Antrim to Wexford, the sun steals
over the shore's grey hem. It is July,
and people wake to their worlds

in old Viking towns, on estuaries,
in the bright estates that curve like
spines on the edges of towns.

Here is the pace of a summer morning:
a lone walker with dogs on a beach,
new light pouring into the hollows of shells,

along the slow glint of dunes where grasses
dip sculptural and silver. What I want is to know
that this can continue, that other mornings

I remember as folds and bolts
of light, the shouting and crosshatch
of bird annunciations, the rustle

of small animals as they move back
for another day in a burrow's darkness,
will stay safe. Is it a question of time?

The atmosphere is thinner, earth threadbare
from a steady weave of hands and neurons
as we make space for millions, while icecaps

melt and deserts spread like spilled ochre.
This morning, those yellows fall moistly
on the shorelines, light has pushed

across hills, through the tillage-acred fields
of Kildare, flashing the duns and greys of horses
riding out at the Curragh's long acres,

on, on to the bog's wild cottons,
stirring larks, a lone heron holding taut
in a meditation of water, a flash of young trout.

Finally, the Shannon is lit, cataracts and bubbles
brighten through the West and its days
of shifting emigrants, students, hopes

of dolphins drawing them home as if to healing.
From Antrim to Wexford, sun has spilt
across the sleeping island, till Galway, Limerick

steady themselves into full colour, as I once
steadied myself when I was ten and watched
an orchard brightening, seized my day.

And now. Another July.
We are waking and working to our worlds,
what is known and unknown,
the world still mine.

FOREST, SNOW, A TRAIN

On the journey from Falun, farmstead roofs
pulled down the snow, their shoulders
tucking white sheets
around ledges and barn doors.

The train hissed along the forest edge.
Daily sleet slopped in headlines against the glass,
became a television from the 60s
lined with interference, sky, snow, tree,
sky, snow, tree, and the houses – yellow or red –
whooped a morse code of comfort. Once, the forest
called out to the train, stop, for heaven's sake, stop!,
but the crystal weighted spruces were swallowed
by horizontal lines, the day's deepening hurry.
          And it would not stop.

The forest's sharp nose was sniffing our warmth,
old bones at the edge of a clearing clicked
with the need for flesh, our blood,
a fire for the coming night.
The train pushed on, and the trees larruped
windy meltings as the carriage sheared south.

On overhead racks, wrapped gifts
of Swedish glass seemed glib,
artifacts in ice, small candles,
and berried woollen hats and gloves
for those who waited,
          at home in the dark.

CONSUMING PASSIONS

My mother preferred home-made cranberry sauce.
Every year I refused her, drove out to country markets
for someone else's pot, passed it off as my own.
To lie was easier, especially in December.

But the Christmas family-party
is not a mere assemblage of relations,
got up at a week or two's notice.

Mother's puddings were in the larder by Halloween,
inoculated with brandy, Schnapps, Fortnum and Mason
fruits and peculiar mutterings
that were a version of her love.

On Christmas Eve, grandmama is in excellent spirits,
and after employing all the children in stoning the plums,
insists on Uncle George stirring the pudding.

But the December before my father's cancer
finally devoured him, my parents' spirits were raucous,
the dining-room ceiling collapsed,
the oven went out and we wept silently together.

It's perfectly delightful, nothing goes wrong,
everybody is in the best of spirits, and disposed
to please and be pleased.

I forgot how much I loved our home,
its ritual of visitors sipping whiskey, a turkey
hung above the white sink in the pantry,
how our parents were once young and joyful,
bolting towards Christmas like horses to a fresh field,

Then the dessert! – and the wine! – and the fun!

THE COSMOS TICKED SILENTLY
(CHRISTMAS, 2013)

They came with fragments hacked from arid inland
    ravines, golden brown or flecked like a pink moon
before a storm. They crammed it before the journey, in a casket.
    Naturally, other gifts – gold, myrrh, some balming oils
for the spent sack of the mother's belly – were brought
    to the narrow refuge where the new family huddled
beside asses, some ailing sheep, one wild dog
    drawn to the smell of birth blood. Steam from bestial
droppings rose in the night. But the al-luban from Oman was
    so fragrant. Even before it burned, the young pair,
exhausted after the journey, stirred, felt purposeful again,
    the future grisling and gurning as the mother marvelled
at the child's nudging lips, his tiny fists that opened and closed
    like desert anemonae. Overhead, a bright, steering cosmos
ticked silently, the enveloping dark pricked with light years
    of stars, indifferent to it all.

One January, the whole country turns to photography. Those without power-cuts chill white wine in the snow on New Year's Day. All the way to the Dublin mountains, a day dressed in white fields, caterpillar hedges, birches held to silence.

A month named after Janus, guardian of doorways, gates, and beginnings. Look back, friend, to a world lying fallow, then forward to spring's slippery sap, the spout and leak of it. wherever leaf and purple and acid yellow whistle out. And even so, the chance of storm and rain, or pearl-grey skies, the trickle-sound of earth, when robins, sparrows and the Kildare crows infiltrate the day.

Later, the Anglo-Saxons call it Wolf Month after the starving wolves raid villages in winter. Hibernating animals still sleep. Plants rest. Only the nunnish Snowdrop pushes thrilling, modest head through chill soil, the centre sparked with threads of yellow. If the winter is mild, daffodils and outdoor hyacinths nudge up in spikes –like the 'fragrance'of the first line of a Haiku poem. Yet they never unsheathe themselves too soon. For such lust, it must be March, and regal with yellowness.

January is a mirror, an ice-pond, a ghost at noon. There is the possibility of oneness but also of detachment from tribal celebration. The wheel of life offers the solace of eventual rest. This is a rehearsal. If I want to celebrate, there's always Little Christmas, or Women's Christmas. It coincides with the Christian Epiphany which marks the visit of the Magi to the child Jesus. The Hindu term Darsana is also connected to 'epiphany', visions of the divine.

The first month hovers beyond the temporal. The sun has passed through the winter solstice and earth has begun its upwards tilt to light. Whatever is in shade seems darker; what is in light, flares with colour. The branches of the birch are like the hull of a boat, strong, curving broadly, the bark mottled with ochre and grey; the oak is sturdy, branches still decked with Christmas lights that flicker softly in the breeze. These trees are enshrouded, have nothing to say, beyond *endure, endure.*

Never look back for long. Memory is too tricky a guide. I live within the short cycle of light, and the alchemy of sloe gins in the evening. Each day, every hour, a minute, a second inscribes itself on me. Time's emissary is calling; but I too inscribe in return: the sense of myself passing through, the sense of my labours in time, in a specific place in this chill, Northern hemisphere, and the clarity that this sometimes brings.

HUSH NOW, IT'S JANUARY

We curl like exhausted lions
in the lair of the house,
make thin journeys for milk, newspapers,

despite the sales. Sheer skies
keep us in the lane, the house frowning
with snow-browed eaves.

Trees also rest, earth's concentrating
philosophers; guardians of sap
reading trickles in matted tunnels,

moss-blanketed. Once, we spy
the sun's hem, avert our eyes religiously.
No rush at all, we drowse,

just the hush of questions, the moment
before, together, after, a drawn breath.
We prepare to live, again obedient

to the call, despite a chill wind
bringing too much savage
laughter about nothing in particular.

came to me in stamps.
"Magyar Posta" ice-skaters, delicate
as Empire porcelain, a fish, an astronaut
and rocket, a silvery boy on 1960s skis.
I understood only difference.
Now, flying home from Budapest,
I touch the pages of my poems, freshly minted
in translation. Now I really don't get them,
but did I ever? The words will make me
briefly native to a coffee-slugging morning reader
on the Vaci Ut, who may not understand,
even in his own tongue.
The lines blur as night slips
through the tilting crowded cabin. Again
I press fingers to page, blind, as if by touch
I could capture a fish, an astronaut, a rocket,
or those elegant, ice-cutting skaters.
Outside, clouds I cannot see
busily translate country to country.

Manoli says the farmers are not sentimental.
The chained fawn dog guards the house, watches
what moves within the mists, his ears like pinnacles.
If the sun flares on a wet stone, he barks.
If the farmer's granddaughter exclaims at new lambs,
his ears swallow her voice, he barks thrice, then stops.
She speaks to her grandfather in the mother tongue.
Manoli says that once they go to school,
they lose the words. The fawn dog watches cyclists,
children, sheep, caped men bound for Finisterre,
frustrated by those with permission to walk.
Around him, the world gulps some words, vomits others.
He knows his place. He knows he has no say.

THE PARTS

Waxen parts observed in the Ethnographic Museum, Santiago de Compostela, Spain

Let us collect a waxen body part
from the corner-shop just after dawn
before the newspapers are delivered.

An arm for you, a hip for me,
a heart for him, phallus, breast
or tongue. Even if we no longer

believe in a god, and no one in their right mind
believes there is a celestial form
which our ailments will fit,

for the cure of misdreamt bodies,
let us take the waxen parts of the old aunt's
failing limbs, the claw of her paralysed

arm, her frozen right leg,
trembling bottom lip, a tongue
which forgets to close off saliva.

Take her wheelchair also.
It has absorbed the illness,
needs molecular healing.

Take a daughter's S-shaped spine,
the scar tissue on her left lung,
let us bear the knots of the fish-monger's arthritis,

his pinched feet and short, hot tendons,
lay them in wax on an operating table,
where belief in a god is not required.

Take our parts in wax. Lay them
as a sign that multitudinous fragments –
hanging hearts and phalluses, used-up wombs,

legs, arms and spines – may despite all rise as one,
to be read and marvelled at
even before the newspapers are delivered.

BABY BOY, QUARYAT AL BERI

They have left him by my sun-bed,
asleep in the shade. His fists are scrolls,
eyelashes dense fluttering fans.
His chest barely moves.

Mother and grandmother test the shallows
of the inlet, their garments spreading darkly.
They dip and manoeuvre, like giant jellyfish.

The young mother smiles back as I peer
at her sleeping son. She senses the waft
of approval, that easy seduction, a baby
settled in the globe of another woman's gaze.

But she cannot know the rest:
my imagining of her son, his future privilege.
No matter how lowly his birth,
there will be women yet lower.

My wary watch softens towards his tight,
creamy fists, the quivering brown lashes,
that incipient dark brow, eyelids
sealed against all divisions,

the hustle, the weighty conscriptions
of his future – to Allah,
to another version of this-god,
that-god, whatever-god, sun,
moon, crescent and sickle, myriad
universes, all newly exploded stars,
all that he may believe as his by right.

A BOY IN GAZA

Will he remember how his sister dragged him
from the street just after the explosion,

how, running, she carried him through rubble?
Eyes wide, her legs stretched in flight

as she leaped across smashed melons, pulped figs
and open-mouthed, still faces. In the photo, her brother's

trousers are stained with blood spatters,
dust, her hair is a nest above her ears, grey

with exploded particles. One arm clenches
his small body against her hip as she

races for their lives, agile
as a fleeing deer from a flaming forest,

her right foot frozen forever, poised in flight,
not yet grounded as she avoids

broken dervishes of mothers, men bawling
like beasts for one another, for their children.

She avoids too the flown daggers of wood
that could pinion her flesh or his

if she puts one foot wrong.
Will he remember his fleeing sister?

WICKLOW

Dedicated to Deirdre Jacobs, Annie McCarrick, Jo-Jo Dollard, Marioara Rostas and the many missing women buried in Wicklow and Irish midlands.*

Up here, a skyful of air and no sound.
This is the safest place, their hidey-hole
and dumping ground, so deep, so dark.
This is where they park, then leave no trace,
depart again with bats and bricks, fists, hammers,
chisels. One way or another, it is all about silence.

And when a storm surges on the mountain,
it's still about silence and claws of lightning
that strike and split a tree, an upright post
in a sloping field of sheep.

The next morning, worms of light
wriggle through heather, fondle globes of dew.
Deer graze in the valley, streams overrun banks,
spread silver cloaks along the grass,
as if this was the garden of innocence.
Deeper still, the big house at Luggala,
a falconry, another cloud-dark lake,
hours spent with tasselled birds
on the long rein, haughty queen kestrels,
out and back, grasping for fresh meat
to tear, devour.

But up high, cars drone the night
beyond Sally Gap, higher, more distant,

---

* The body of Rumanian-born Marioara Rostas was recovered. During the trial, one witness described how he and his companion danced on her body when they threw it in the grave However, as the witness was considered unreliable by the jury, his evidence was discounted and the alleged killer remains free.

drive steadily through the dun light.
Fog rolls across waiting slopes
when they decide to dig, to bury,
to sometimes dance on a nuisance grave,
above the body of the woman they want rid of.

For this is the safest place, their hidey-hole
and dumping ground, so deep, so dark.
One way or another, it is all about silence.

WOMAN OF MY DREAMS

Time noses mole-like, passing or ignoring
what once seemed the drama of the day.
I wonder about my fuss and battle,
would restart conversations short circuited

by my need to star-shoot with her son,
to stub her motherhood underfoot
because I was his wife. No longer
daughter-in-law to mother-in-law;

prescriptions of age, position, gender,
long met, I would meet and speak
of matters beyond our interest:
her son – my husband, our child –

her granddaughter. I would place those fetishes
of female division within a closed cell,
then throw away the key to hear her speak
of Yorkshire and the moors, girl-scouts,

Sheffield and the Blitz. I would listen
with purer hearing for her stories,
than when my ears waxed like moons in my head,
straining in her direction – the enemy –

yet caught within the cyclical need
to be the free woman of my dreams.
In mortal combat with myself, I fought with her
in silence. But the evening before she slipped

camp grounds, she did not know me, or anyone –
her eyes were fretless skies – no cloud, no heather,
no ground to fix the feet. Female fetishes long laid to rest,
I saw at last a very old woman.

And myself: those old moons on the wane,
no longer baleful, and thinking well of her.

WAITING OUTSIDE BEWLEYS

At that doorway how often have I glided,
smooth-hipped through crowds to see my mother wait
with glossy packages on looped string.

She never recognised me until
I was before her, but pretended. 'I saw you,'
she proclaimed, 'You move like a hot knife

through butter!' And once, grandmother's shoe-heel
snagged on the café stairs, and she fell.
We helped her up, reassembled her country dignity.

Yesterday, I lolled in soft paws of coffee air, just beside
the counter. Shoppers streamed, magazine-sellers
changed coins, the bells of Clarendon St Church

rang out, so that I, distracted, did not see
this daughter hot-knife her way along until
she pulled up short before me, loops of hair

damp with drizzle as she smiled. Was she Grace
or Fate? What half-remembered female from
the staircase of the past now gazed from her eyes

at me? Inside, we ordered buns and coffee,
settled down to pass the fragments of our stories,
mouths generating some sweeter recognition,

not just icing.

SISTER-TRADE

Three days with you and I smoke in sisterhood
although I hardly inhale; three days and we
exchange clothes and perfume samples, trade

gifts and impulses – as if to deeply fill the trench
that once separated us, bedding it down with thoughts
of what might please the other. How quaint.

How Elizabeth Barrett Browning, I sometimes think:
those hours of gifting one another small memories,
feeling elements of what he said or did, how she

delighted in your note-perfect memory of Mozart's
Alleluia at the age of three. You were the genius,
it was thought. I might have been Salieri, except

for the way the sun fell on both our lives, and shadows
stretched, shifting the light from your landscape. Even so.
There are cigarettes, clothes, our conversations,

a prosecution of place and time, the lovely house
and our galloping parents, bound as much as us now,
with secrets – unknowable, ours alone.

THE WIGS

She told me the tale of fair Rapunzel,
who unpinned her hair so the prince could twist
his ankle around her strands and climb the casement.
Sometimes, I played with her hair, carefully,
so as not to snag it, drew the thick tumble

through a wooden-backed long brush that crackled
with electricity, teased waves to ringlets.
She wore her hair longer than other women,
fair-flooded, letting it out with the pulse
of her charm. When psoriasis flowered in flakes

on her scalp, the hair fell in wisps to the floor,
squeezed from its keratinoid armour,
indifferent to brushes and lacquers, first,
timid hairpieces. In the end, a catalogue
promised the solution: battle not over,

the wigs arrived. Some she draped on the heads
of Derbyshire figurines and on door-handles,
yet others found their way to settle on chairs,
like tight-curled cats asleep in shafts of light.
Beautiful, renewed, sometimes fretting about

high winds, blizzards, the demon weather that
could undo her, revealing shame – her pate,
the lonely fate of having no power
to let down, nor prince to climb that edifice,
his feet entwined in lustrous strands, as he

reached the narrow casement to enter that
dark room, where a prudent woman once spun
a yarn as long as hair, signalled in a mother's
telling voice, when to unpin your head,
and what it meant.

EDEN

Someone long ago had planted Beauty of Bath
in the Protestant orchard of my childhood.
My mother's orchard. Insects devoured that neglected
sweetness she never saw as she drove out, forgetful
of us as we lounged in the crotches of old trees,
emperors, surviving wars. We did battle with nettles,
cock-chafers and frogs, wary of Devil's Coachman
and a local myth of vipers. We were the cousins,
knowledgeable and ready as troops on the march,
with dogs for elephants. Sometimes fear set us back,
until someone became an Alexander, play-acting courage
to keep the troops in the mood. Ahead lay our India –
bejewelled apple-trees, the potioned poms, flesh creamy
and flush-veined. We found mouth-rubies on which to gorge,
new maps to the senses, an antidotal release
on our tongues – luscious, forbidden – priming us.

At thirty-five thousand feet, I cannot sleep.
No pill or drink abolishes this dense night
though both are melting on my tongue.
We drift alone in the high metal hull
of a spectral ship, the blood in our veins sluggish.
Ropes cut, anchors raised, I know with certainty
that I am cast off from a world so cruel
yet so loved for its tiny harbours of mercy.

My eye seeks winking villages across Mongolia,
Siberia, any wavering signal from the ground.
Virus flowering lights spread around St. Petersburg,
the night in thick pursuit as we tilt south,
as if starving wolves and possessing djinns
had risen from some remote Silesian village.
Then a long bridge between Sweden, Denmark,
and we are falling, falling, bellies register
the gravity and pull of this descent
to the rumpled world, towards the English coast,
shrouded fields. Finally, the snuff-marks and electricity
of London, wheels drop and a grey band of runway
beckons, welcomes an end of journeys,
before the final trawl to Ireland. Two hours later,
I press another calming pill, its dry melt on my tongue
as Dublin spreads its limbs, swallows me whole.

DUBLIN

I still wonder why I stayed.
It slid its streets around my waist,
old boy of the black pool,
whispered riddles from the cobbles,

rose to my ear till I was dazed with secrets,
The river edged the spring nights
with stinking sludge, rough braiding at low tide
when the sea rushed to consume the filth.

Buddleia sprouted high up in derelict Georgians
along the quays, wind-waving as the buses
lurched towards Half-penny Bridge.
And still it poured sweet-talk and nothings.

But my feet became Dublin feet,
tramping streets from Parnell to Molesworth
bearing banners to wave at presidents,
the heels of our boots gritty, voices

outraged, as we crossed O'Connell.
With room to breathe, I lost myself
in the peace of the crowd. It offered
gift on gift in quayside junk-shops,

plied me till I was absorbed, tricks
like a 1900s photograph album
bought for a pound beneath wavering
Christmas lights, the cover gold-scrolled,

an Edwardian family's passage
from Westland Row* to Burma.

* Dublin railway station now called Pearse.

I study them in sepia, seated beside trunks
before the boat-train to Dun Laoghaire

buttoned and hatted, their travel finery
and sturdy shoes flashed-forward to memory
for an album not yet made.
To think it was thrown out, that chronicle

of their time in high foreign fields,
women playing lacrosse in loose skirts,
or once, seated beneath the tamarinds
while tea was served, their blonde children

and unsmiling native nannies
close to hand. This Christmas, I pledge
myself a vanished family's keeper,
protect some remnant of its men

and women, who ensured the camera
would record those steaming nights,
malarial, those tropical gins
with no ice, women bored and far

from the hum of home, the rain-glossed
Dublin trams hissing and rattling
through wistful dreams as the monsoon poured.
The place they lost still slides its streets around me,

all wiles, whispers from the cobbles,
perfumes my ear till I am dazed.
It never failed me, the old boy, though
I often wondered why I stayed.

AN IRISH LEXICON

(A, B, C, D, E, F, G, H, I, L, M, N, O, P, R, S, T, U)*

Twilight, and the deer are grazing in the Phoenix Park.
Someone dreams of Arkle, Beara, Drumlins, Errigal.
A poet writes of Dubh Linn, Lonndubh, Belfast,

Glens of Imal, Antrim, The Downs,
Devil's Bit, Vinegar Hill, The Hook, Bannow,
Ships, helmets, Ogham, Newgrange,

Dawn chorus, dawn light, grave passages,
Burren limestone, dolmen, capstone, and Dowth.
In school they speak of Flight, Grammar, Imram,

Lir, Marian, Naoise, Oriel, in the Dáil it's Partnership,
Rights, salmon, Taoiseach / Toscairí.
Sea fog and frost are rolling in. Land holds its breath.

✠

The SOMEONE, the TEACHER, the POET,
the POLITICIAN weave a dialogue of badger-bait,
bull-bait, dog-fight, and greyhound,
Cú, Cuchullan, Dun Dealgan, Eamhain Macha,
Tháinig long ó Valparaiso, tá tír na n-óg
Ag cúl an tí, tir alainn trina céile,
Mise Eire, Micheal Ó Suilleabhán,
The Long Hall, The Brazen Head, The Oliver
St. John Gogarty, The South Pole Inn, Omagh bomb,
Gugán Barra, Guests of the Nation, La Mon,
Oedipus Complex, Lough Swilly, Anna Livea,
National Museum, Síle na Gig, jigs and reels,

* The Irish language alphabet has only 18 letters.

65

Riverdance, Liberty Hall, the Limerick pogrom of 1904,
the bee-loud glade, the beehive hut, Georgian Dublin,
Liberty Hall rebuilt and scaling the clouds,
Custom House, Guinness, the fighting boys of Annabelle's,
Fairview Park, The George, Dawn Run, the Curragh.

Wren Women, Glencree, Synagogue, Germans and Jews,

Wicklow Jail, ghosts, Kilmainham,
Dawn executions in Dublin,
the Disappeared, Jean McConville, 1994, Abercorn, poteen,
the Black Pig's Dyke, De Valera, Crazy Jane,
Old Croghan Man at rest in the his glass box,
clean as a newborn, renewed for viewing by millions.
Arigna, slit nipples, The Clonskeagh Mosque,
laundries, the Imam, Good Shepherd Convent,
CPRSI, Bessborough, the Protestants of Cork in 1921,
Monaghan 1974, Belfast Agreement, Fish on Friday,
Good Friday Agreement, that blackbird over Emy Lough,
gold at Clontibret, ghost estates in Laois, a haunted house
in Lucan, golden apples of the sun, whatever-you-say,
oil off Cork, Daghda, the Boyne, UB-65,
September 1913, extra points for Honours Maths,
Gaelscoileanna, Bodhráns and spoons,harp-making
in Portlaoise jail, piebalds in Jobstown, free buggies
for immigrants, free curtains, money-for-old-rope-
single-mothers-of-four, Arkle, Beara, a wherewithal
for bags of coal, turf, as a wretched frost descends.

And yet we have a fabled coast, where sea-cattle plunge
into the WAVES. Inland, hill-sprites on DRUMLINS,
pismires on the bog, all CELT and tribe in South Ulster,
further north there's ERRIGAL, but speak not,
SAY-NOTHING, for words will never count so much as
gesture.

Flight of the Earls, O'Neill in Rome, Michael Robartes,
Kenny in D.C., Irish artists in New York,
Bringing-It-All-Over-There, the knowledge,
the Gathering, the sliver of salmon, the sucked thumb,
Fairtrade, Taltainn, free-range eggs, free-loaders,
curlews, buzzards, Lissadell.

Twilight, and the deer are grazing in the Phoenix Park.
Someone dreams of Arkle, Beara, Drumlins, Errigal.
On the Curragh, whin bushes dream, and horses
are stabled for the night. Frost bites down.

✠

CELTS

The exotic myth of origin, spread its cloak
from Eire to Scotland, Wales, Brittany, Galicia.
Even today, defies the MONGREL MIX.

I'm an Irishwoman (*you're Irish? I love*
the way you people speak!). Then part Scotwoman,
part Norman-maid, part O'Donnell on the way home
from KINSALE, some fragment of embattled clan,
lingering in Limerick, not a Donegal gene in my bones.

IT DOES NOT MATTER, WHAT WE FORGET,
AND MYTH IS NOT EXOTIC, (in text-speak this is
SHOUTING, but to stretch the letters high,
to break the stifled code of poetries on the Island
of the Mongrel Mixture of frayed saints and devils.
Search for scholars. All gone to homes
in America's universities. The saying used to go,
'At least, we're not British' as the gombeen men

set up their 70s supermarket empires in ribboning
suburbs, ran despite themselves away from rural,
Catholic, the West, in denial until Robinson
hit the Presidency: how we rejoiced at her inauguration,
at the chewed-wasp faces of Lenihan and Haughey.

But in denial till then,
I AM *A* BECAUSE I AM NOT *B*. I AM IRISH
BECAUSE I AM NOT BRITISH

☩

MÁTHAIR MO CHROÍ*

Front line of the defence, a line with no power
unless in the home, twisting sons into priests,
daughters to carers like themselves. Mine simmered.
EDUCATION! she cried, IT'S CARRIED
LIGHTLY ALL YOUR LIFE, MY DAUGHTERS.
In old age, educated, with three university
degrees, her modesty comes from knowing
we know nothing when facts are put to bed,
and all that's left is the heart-thorn of experience,
although she does not refuse her haute couture,
smudge-pot colours brightening her eyes at eighty-seven,
alive and equivocating to the end, but moved
by *The Deer's Cry*, *The Fox-Hunt*,
music from the culture dancing in her soul.

Mise Eire and O'Riada once strung and boomed
through the house of my girlhood, between Acker Bilk

---

* Literally, 'mother of my heart', this is a common cliché derived
from traditional songs and poems in Ireland.

and Renata Tebaldi. Music, she said,
WAS PORTAL TO THE SOUL.
And so she taught her daughters, guiltless.

✠

MISE LE MEAS*

Everybody knew the telephone girls listened in.

You had to be careful what you said, and women
having affairs around the town learned fast.
The phone was not safe, and the local MI5
custodians of half-baked morality liked to chatter.
But this was Monaghan. Nobody had affairs
in the 1960s, did they? Nobody committed suicide,
did they? Nobody was gay. Some parents
had a copy of TANTRIC SEX, beside
THE CATHOLIC MARRIAGE, secreted in the high
wardrobe, and Mary McCarthy a presence
in that east-facing bedroom, where my parents could see
foxes at play in the high field,
beyond wind-tilted knots of holly trees.

But the telephone girls, those telephone girls,
how they tattled in the town! They knew
who owed what to whom, who in HIGH POWER
was doing his secretary, and the garda known
to lightly squeeze a woman's breast, great paw

---

* The official way of signing off a Government letter, it means 'Yours,
respectfully' but even today is associated with indifference, anonym-
ity and unaccountability.

in through the car window as he advised her
on traffic conditions.

Hear them, that Irish sibilance: *Putting you through now*
Hello Clones, call for you ...ah how are ya Elsie, not a bad day,
yesterday was pure shockin'... right now, call waiting
Caller? Putting you through now...

✠

REBUKE TO IDEOLOGICAL FEMINISTS

"I was not one of the popular feminists who knew what a sound-
bite was... never took the Contraceptive Train north* nor went to
Greenham Common..." – the poet, 2013

We never moved as one, ladies, girls, women,
to suggest that it was otherwise would be a lie.
Today, some of you are CIVIL as any servant,
as IVORY-TOWERED as any ruminating scholar,
as unsmiling, grim and frightening as women would be
who thirty years ago spent time contemplating cervixes,
took classes in How Not to Smile All the Time.
Too much smiling – agreed – too much compliance
and willingness. You can be anyone you want!
Self-invent, renaissance women all!
We'll help you on the way to smash that glass ceiling!

(*If we are to believe the weekly* Elle, *the woman of letters is a remarkable*
Zoological species: she brings forth, pell-mell, novels and children.

* 'The Contraceptive Train', as it was known, was boarded in Dublin's
Connolly Station in 1971 by a group of feminists who then travelled to
Belfast to buy contraceptives that were at that time illegal in the Repub-
lic. They then returned that afternoon and brandished their purchases,
daring the Customs Officials to challenge them.

We are introduced, for example, to Jacqueline Lenoir (two daughters, one novel); Marina Grey (one son, one novel); Nicole Dutreil (two sons, four novels), *etc*).

But what does it mean? *This: to write
is a glorious but bold activity; the writer is an 'artist',
one recognises that he is entitled to a little bohemianism**...

Even so. It does not include the ordinary women
getting on with ordinary lives, the ones who wrestle
infant feet into little shoes, who wipe up puke, wipe shitty bums,
clean the rooms where some of you work out the policies.
*But make no mistake: Let no women believe
that they can take advantage of this pact without having first
submitted to the eternal statute of womanhood.
Women are on the earth to give children to men;
let them write as much as they like, let them decorate
Their condition, but above all, let them not depart from it*...

Some of you never recognised that we were not so helpless,
despite biology, so victimised, or speechless,
nor saw that we were ON YOUR SIDE.

The suspicion often fell that *this* was how you wanted it:
you, on the band-wagon, questioning the language
(*that* remains a GOOD IDEA).

*A careful analysis of the teacher-student relationship
at any level, inside or outside the school, reveals
its fundamentally narrative character. This relationship*

* From Roland Barthes, *Mythologies*, Editions du Seuil, 1957, Paris.

involves a narrating Subject (the teacher) and patient, listening objects (the students)*.

The sexuality, the *mode d'emploi* of every bloody thing not quite your business. Your business was – is – JUSTICE, FAIRNESS, HUMAN RIGHTS, not CONDESCENSION AND KNOWING WHAT WAS BETTER FOR YOUR MINIONS.

The battle goes on – ladies, girls, women. The principle remains correct and this enquiry asks that you get your hands dirtied in the ordinary smut, break your own networks and move into the favellas, the country, wherever the road is twisted and UNTHINK IS IN CHARGE, get working with the people, SEE WHERE JUSTICE IS DONE and learn from that. Or: remember Orwell, that thing about everyone being equal, But some are...? He got it right, all charged up with a memory of native male backsides skinned by the bamboo rod, released from prison to impoverished wives who soothed it all with mashed banana. M – A – S – H – E – D   B – A – N – A – N - A .

✠

So Unthink the Englishmen were let loose.
But to each generation its Unthinks. Unthink the Nation, the State, the Federation, the Republic, the Monarchy, the Commune, the Parish, the County, the GAA, League, Union, Association, Gathering, Meeting, in every unstarry constellation where people meet there's a Mr. Unthink, partnered by Ms Unthink and all the Littler Unthinkums.

* Paolo Freire, *Pedagogy of the Oppressed*, Penguin Education, 1972.

All Unthinking how they need LOVE, how LOVE rules the world,
how LOVE is everything and we surely ALL LOVE one another,
thee-most-bee-ewt-iful-word in thee world! But the same one
all the same for man-woman, mother-child, child-parent,
bro and sis, covering the spectrum as if it were one colour.

It ain't one colour Ma'ams: it's not black, it's not white,
it's all and any hut, it hides so deeply it's like Mars the planet,
people wondering if there ever was life, and if liquid water
ever flowed in that barren territory. That's what LOVE is.

And then love flows into politics. Into ideals. Into agendas.

Enter: Stage Right: The Leader of the Women's Forum
presides at her Constituency, plus Chief Female Poets,
addressing the great iambed on cross-rhyme
and good-tempered rhyme, Being one's Own Best Critic,
and Seizing Permissions.

Stampede Stage Left: the confused massing women,
their fret and fever about window cleanliness,
toilet-bowls, children and curries.
Until: behind them,
a quieter entering: the old, the weak,
the sick, the confused, the mad, the neurotic, the demented:
such fill the stage, while behind them again serried lines
of workers, bee-women, the soft hum of labour, creased brow,
compliant to the nature of life's business:
love of the task that transforms.
The only love, perhaps.

✠

73

Twilight, and the deer are grazing in the Phoenix Park.
Someone dreams of Arkle, Beara, Drumlins, Errigal.
A poet writes of Dubh Linn, Lonndubh, Belfast,

Glens of Imal, Antrim, The Downs,
Devil's Bit, Vinegar Hill, The Hook, Bannow,
ships, helmets, Ogham, Newgrange,

Dawn chorus, dawn light, grave passages,
Burren limestone, dolmen, capstone, and Dowth.
Whin bushes on the Curragh toss and dream

as the wind untethers them. Horses are stabled
for the night. A fox runs close to the ditch,
beyond the steady shearing of evening cars, headlights.

Frost trembles on the air, falls firm across the land,
cooling an ardour of wintry argument.
The earth rounds in on its prayer to itself.

BOUTIQUE HOTEL

Cardiff, 2010

It was once an office building.
Boys and girls came and went,
after leaving school, before marriage.
There were fixed terms at type-writers,
where IBM Golfballs spun and hammered,
or in accounts with hand-inscribed ledgers.

They took coffee-breaks beneath the Styrofoam
tile ceiling, gossiped, nail-chewing
at the prospect of some unhappy
Thunder Face, his passive-aggressive memos
to do this, have that done by yesterday,
yesterday.

It once had bathrooms on every floor,
where each sex released its stream
into ceramic vessels, enjoyed
peace and privacy, the ocean-hiss
of cisterns and wash-basins,
taking time to recover from life hours

pissed away in service. Some girls prayed
for the sight of menstrual blood,
fixed holes in tights with clear nail-polish,
stretched mouths wide at mirrors, self-testing
on a socially agreed smileometer.
Now, it's a retro inn at fifty quid a night,

in Sixties psychedelic pinks and yellows,
walls endorsed by shots of a sinister
Hollywood actor, corridors
threaded alive with young voices,
yellow-haired Japanese, a trio of Germans,
mouths full, fingers sticky with Danish pastries.

And me: nesting for the night in a bed
huge as a jetty over a green lake.
I float beneath Styrofoam skies,
think of girls like me
who once roved Carnaby Street
in an Afghan coat, wanting to be Twiggy,

to know McLaren – any Kink would do
at a Waterloo Sunset – among summer crowds,
the hot, exhausted city,
but instead the pink pearl in my crotch,
beneath a chambermaid's uniform,
ached, lust-drenched.

FIVE A.M.

Your eyelids tear open like unpeeling glue.
A room takes shape. Monochrome curtain,
but radiance in glass candlesticks
that glint and wink along the sill.

Later the kitchen also takes shape,
a mood has evolved. You stand erect,
your arms fill kettle, fingers push bread in toaster,
thumbs push the lid of the Marmite jar.

Other rooms assume form,
you surge with post-breakfast capability,
stroke the spines of books, pause
on the landing to check the prophecy of light
from the mountains.

In the bathroom, you squeeze tubes, open jars,
toss careless towel, find comfort
in black and white tiles,
set and geometric in pure northern light.

The many walls of the house of the self
now flex, graduate to colour.
They come full focus as if brushed
to a bloom of scarlet flush, sea green stairway
and the white passage hallway
playing with fingers of light.

Outside, you pull and push –
drift past field and road,
to city's tidal river surging to sea.
Soon, you are resurrected, transfigured
from the razor edge of five a.m.,
this precarious life.

OLD CROGHAN MAN KNOCKING AT THE WINDOW

*The bog body of what is now called Old Croghan Man was found in
a bog beneath Croghan Hill in County Offaly. Based on radiocarbon
dating he died sometime between 362 BC and 175 BC.*

He dined sublimely – elk and venison,
fat cattle grazed on green slopes at forest's edge;
all the help he needed to sow and till,
to hunt with hounds, bring home his pledge

of bounty. But they descended like a pack of wild dogs,
flailed him, then competed for his killing.
Trimmed cuticles and ovoid fingernails,
they left alone. Those fingers knew honour,

not labour; digits flexed to receive lord and crone
alike, to raise a spear, a goblet, a pouch of coins.
They broke everything else in his body: did he shriek
from loss of nerve? Nipples cut, upper arms riven

to thread his pain in hazel withies? Enough torment,
before they severed him in half? Poor king, failed king,
wedded to a harsh goddess of land and war,
No tyrant, this man offended the people's mood,

put tidy fingernails and waxed eyebrows
on the day's agenda, failing them and his goddess.
In rage and famine, the people turned.
At night, his fingernails come tapping

at the window of dreams, the filed strength of them
rhythming down the centuries towards other mens' hearing.
By day, in the glass box of consciousness,
we witness fingers at rest, as if in sleep.

ON FITZWILLIAM, AFTER A BUDGET

1.

Car radios announce the worst.
Tonight in Ireland, people will lie
as we once did, fretting into pillows.
Workers retreat to suburbs,
counting the years, the money, what is lost
to order and effort, recent virtues of this State.

On Fitzwilliam Square, the sky glints blue
through bolts of cloud. Beside the railings,
a couple kiss. He thumbs her jaw-line
as if sculpting her. Her face is pale, upturned,
eyelids shut. Already, they are beyond
the invisible rag and bone stalls,
the money-lenders beckoning.

2.

I remember another budget, when
the long jaw of Haughey pronounced
on the spendthrift masses, who struggled
to divide and expand the indivisible,
and kids ran after coal lorries,
sent to scoop the fallen lumps from roads
of concreted estates.
Our friends departed by the day,
letters from San Francisco, Australia,
anyplace that welcomed their gifts.

I speak of gifts and it is true we had them.
Behind the divide of us and them,
our leaders cackled like the ancient Greeks,

every old-git, lunched-up, farting *turannos*
ripping into the hopeful on a chant of
'too much luxury, tighten your belts!'
We drank thin Chianti, played bohemians
beneath twine lampshades, with occasional weed
to make us feel cool, learned to cook
like Europeans, Asians, anything but Irish.

We stayed, believing we were gifted.
The privilege of nation, hoped in,
treated gently by our like, came to us.
There was no other place.

Thirty years on,
the carcass-rippers maul again,
money-lenders scatter, their coins void.

Yet, like us, that couple on Fitzwilliam
kiss and kiss again, the world's rough edges
briefly smooth as they linger to drift
and pause along the railings,
their eyelids closing out the day.

Someone's scrawled a love-line on the metal shutter –
Moro Luvs Suz. In the rain, my hair
is a cap of dripping ringlets. I wait for battered chicken,
sauces. Outside again, unlock the car with salty fingers.
At the red light I text you about the latest deluge,
the state of your apartment in Inchicore,
trashed by an amazing friend.
I call you in from deserts, from Mexico to the Mojave.

You text in reply: why come back?
Scant pickings here too, just slightly better,
the Salinas fields are unprofitable, the sun astringent,
the laid-off men are cradling heads in arms,
but even so it's warmer. You're riding it out
near the Plazas or at Hillcrest,
where we once posed outside a tranny shop,
the hot nipples of our cigarettes defiant. Your boss

has died of lymphoma, Betty Ann consoles you
when the arid evenings prowl, and you long
for the bite of a cold beer, the intricate lace of vodka
dressing your gut – or gin, or ten Tequilas.
At home, nightmares stroll in broad daylight:
the lingering heroic, occasional as poems, stern
as Lady Gaga's voice, a hammer-tong of notes
tosses her ponytail, drives some

to think about futures perfect. The rest make ready
to lie down, cradle their lives in arms as if settling
for a blizzard. No riots here, but patriotic geeks-in-arms.
Let's tweet about Byzantium, what we might do
when out of body and intensity has died.
Let's tweet till our fingers are worn to stubs,
about high, roaring fires, foxgloves and roses

on an evening porch, let's tweet about the things recalled:
those clanking tills, the halfpence too,
we never really wanted that, our vivid faces
betraying a mess where the golden-gated,
stoney-eagled still live on, protected from our wrath.

MARY O'DONNELL has published six previous poetry collections, the most recent of which, *The Ark Builders*, is from Arc – as well as four novels and two collections of short fiction. Her poetry is widely published in journals and anthologies both in Europe and in the USA and most recently her selected poems appeared in a prize-winning Hungarian edition with Irodalmi Jelen (translator Tamas Kabdebo). She is co-editor of *To the Winds Our Sails* (2010), an anthology of Galician women's poetry in translation.

A regular contributor of radio essays to Ireland's national broadcaster, RTE, she teaches part-time on Carlow University Pittsburgh's MFA in Creative Writing at Trinity College Dublin. In 2001, she was elected to the membership of the artists' academy Aosdána.

Further information: www.maryodonnell.com

Selected titles in Arc Publications'
POETRY FROM THE UK / IRELAND include:

LIZ ALMOND
The Shut Drawer
Yelp!

D. M. BLACK
Claiming Kindred

JAMES BYRNE
Blood / Sugar
White Coins

JONATHAN ASSER
Outside The All Stars

DONALD ATKINSON
In Waterlight:
Poems New, Selected & Revised

ELIZABETH BARRETT
A Dart of Green & Blue

JOANNA BOULTER
Twenty Four Preludes & Fugues on
Dmitri Shostakovich

THOMAS A CLARK
The Path to the Sea

TONY CURTIS
What Darkness Covers
The Well in the Rain
folk

JULIA DARLING
Sudden Collapses in Public Places
Apology for Absence

LINDA FRANCE
You are Her

KATHERINE GALLAGHER
Circus-Apprentice
Carnival Edge

RICHARD GWYN
Sad Giraffe Café

GLYN HUGHES
A Year in the Bull-Box

MICHAEL HASLAM
The Music Laid Her Songs in Language
A Sinner Saved by Grace
A Cure for Woodness

MICHAEL HULSE
The Secret History
Half-Life

CHRISTOPHER JAMES
Farewell to the Earth

BRIAN JOHNSTONE
The Book of Belongings
Dry Stone Work

JOEL LANE
Trouble in the Heartland
The Autumn Myth

HERBERT LOMAS
A Casual Knack of Living
COLLECTED POEMS

SOPHIE MAYER
(O)

PETE MORGAN
August Light

MICHAEL O'NEILL
Wheel
Gangs of Shadow

MARY O'DONNELL
The Ark Builders

IAN POPLE
An Occasional Lean-to
Saving Spaces

PAUL STUBBS
The Icon Maker
The End of the Trial of Man

LORNA THORPE
A Ghost in My House
Sweet Torture of Breathing

ROISIN TIERNEY
The Spanish-Italian Border

MICHELENE WANDOR
Musica Transalpina
Music of the Prophets
Natural Chemistry

JACKIE WILLS
Fever Tree
Commandments
Woman's Head as Jug